My Life with
Diabetes

written by **Mari Schuh** • art by **Ana Sebastián**

AMICUS ILLUSTRATED
is published by Amicus
P.O. Box 227, Mankato, MN 56002
www.amicuspublishing.us

Copyright © 2024 Amicus. International copyright reserved in all countries. No part of this book
may be reproduced in any form without written permission from the publisher.

Editor: Rebecca Glaser
Series Designer: Kathleen Petelinsek
Book Designer: Lori Bye

Library of Congress Cataloging-in-Publication Data
Names: Schuh, Mari C., 1975- author. | Sebastián, Ana, illustrator.
Title: My life with diabetes / by Mari Schuh ; illustrated by Ana Sebastián.
Description: Mankato, Minnesota: Amicus Learning, [2024] | Series: My life with... | Includes bibliographical references.
| Audience: Ages 6–9 | Audience: Grades 2–3 |
Summary: "Meet Tiana! She likes gymnastics, cooking, and drawing. She also has diabetes. Tiana is real and so are her experiences.
Learn about her life in this illustrated narrative nonfiction picture book for elementary students"—Provided by publisher.
Identifiers: LCCN 2022045672 (print) | LCCN 2022045673 (ebook)
| ISBN 9781645494904 (library binding) | ISBN 9781681528977 (paperback) | ISBN 9781645494942 (ebook)
Subjects: LCSH: Diabetics—Juvenile literature.
Classification: LCC RJ420.D5 S36 2024 (print) | LCC RJ420.D5 (ebook) |
DDC 618.92/462—dc23/eng/20221003
LC record available at https://lccn.loc.gov/2022045672
LC ebook record available at https://lccn.loc.gov/2022045673

Printed in China

For Tiana and her family—MS

About the Author
Mari Schuh's love of reading began with cereal boxes at
the kitchen table. Today she is the author of hundreds of
nonfiction books for beginning readers. With each book, Mari
hopes she's helping kids learn a little bit more about the world
around them. Find out more about her at marischuh.com.

About the Illustrator
Ana Sebastián is an illustrator living in Spain. She studied
Fine Arts at University of Zaragoza and Université Michel
de Montaigne, Bordeaux. Specializing in digital illustration,
she completed her education with a master's degree in
digital illustration for concept art and visual development.

Hi there! I'm Tiana. I love to play at the park. At home, I like to draw, cook, and watch videos. I also have diabetes. Let me tell you about my life.

People with diabetes have too much glucose in their blood. Glucose is a type of sugar. The cells use it for energy. A hormone called insulin delivers glucose to the body's cells. When people don't have enough insulin, their blood sugar level rises. This can make a person sick.

Food

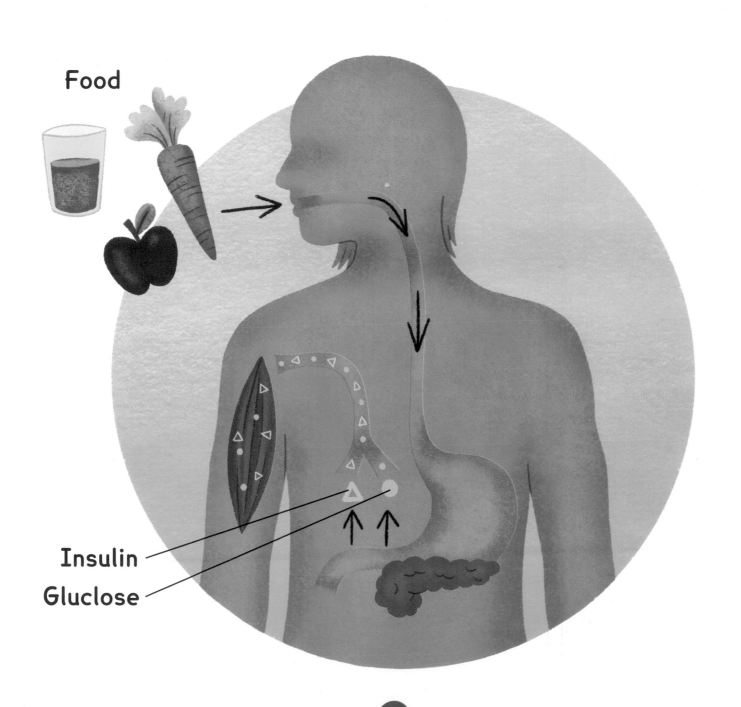

Insulin

Gluclose

I have type 1 diabetes. Kids with diabetes often have type 1. This means my body does not make enough insulin. I need doses of insulin every day. I have a pump on my body. Other people get shots.

My great grandma has type 2 diabetes. This type is more common in adults. Her body makes insulin. But her body can't use it in the right way. She takes medicine to help her.

One day when I was three years old, I was very tired. I was thirsty. I went to the bathroom a lot. My mom took me to the hospital. That's when I found out I have diabetes.

I need to check my blood sugar many times a day. I learned how to do this when I was three. Now that I'm older, it's really easy for me to do. I use a blood glucose meter. It tells me if my blood sugar is too high or too low.

A small pump at my waist gives me insulin all day. It has a tube that goes just under my skin. Some people stare at my pump. That's okay. I tell them how it helps me.

Food, exercise, and insulin affect my blood sugar levels. I try to keep those three things in balance. Before I play, I eat a healthy snack. This keeps my blood sugar from getting too low. When it's low, I feel weak. I get a headache.

I am mindful of what I eat and how much. I read food labels all the time. I can eat some sweets and carbohydrates. But too much makes my blood sugar too high. Then I take more insulin to lower my blood sugar.

Having diabetes can be hard.
I can't go on school field trips
unless an adult goes with me.
Sometimes people think they
can get diabetes from me.
I tell them they can't catch
diabetes from other people.

At meals, people start to eat
right away. But I have to wait
to eat. I need to check my
blood sugar first.

Diabetes is only one part of who I am.
I like to do gymnastics. I like to draw, too.

At school, I love to learn about science. Diabetes doesn't stop me from doing most things. I pay attention to how I feel. I make sure to take good care of myself.

In the summer, I go to diabetes camp. I meet kids who have diabetes just like me. They understand me. They know how I feel.

Having diabetes has helped me to be responsible. I eat healthy food. I remember to check my blood sugar levels.

My mom tells me about famous people who have diabetes. It did not stop them from their goals. It doesn't stop me, either! When I grow up, I want to be a chef. I want to make healthy food for people with diabetes.

Meet Tiana

Hi! I'm Tiana. I live in North Carolina with my family. My hobbies include singing, cooking, and swimming. Playing games on my computer is also fun. I love to dance with my friends. We make up new dance moves. At school, I like to explore new ideas in science class. Art is also one of my favorite classes. I like to draw pictures of people and fairies.

Respecting People with Diabetes

People with diabetes often need to use pumps, shots, and medicine. Don't bully or tease them. Treat them how you would like to be treated.

People with diabetes need to check their blood sugar levels. Don't rush them. Be patient and kind.

If a person with diabetes can't eat the food you want to share, don't pressure them to eat it. They need to stay healthy and safe.

People with diabetes might need to eat a snack before being active. Be sure to be patient and understanding.

Kids with diabetes are like other kids. They want to play and have fun. Ask them to play with you.

A person with diabetes might feel different. Be a good friend to them.

Helpful Terms

blood sugar level The amount of glucose in a person's blood.

carbohydrate A nutrient in foods such as bread, cereal, rice, and potatoes.

dose A measured amount of medicine to be taken at one time.

glucose A type of sugar in a person's blood that the body uses for energy.

hormone A chemical made by a gland in the body that affects the way a person grows and develops.

insulin A hormone that helps the body use sugar for energy. Insulin controls the amount of sugar in a person's blood.

responsible Able to keep promises, follow rules, and do what you say you will do.

Read More

Benson, Jodyanne. **Diabetes.** @RosenTeenTalk. New York: Rosen Publishing, 2021.

Hopkins, Linda K. **Diabetes.** In Case of Emergency. New York: AV2, 2021.

Sipe, Nicole. **Living with Type 1 Diabetes: Understanding Ratios.** Huntington Beach, Calif.: Teacher Created Materials, 2019.

Websites

BBC: LIVING WITH DIABETES: PHOEBE'S STORY

https://www.bbc.co.uk/teach/class-clips-video/primary-pshe-health-diabetes-phoebes-story/zrvr8xs

Seven-year-old Phoebe talks about what it's like to have diabetes.

KIDSHEALTH: DIABETES CENTER FOR KIDS

https://kidshealth.org/en/kids/center/diabetes-center.html

Get tips on staying healthy and coping if you have diabetes.

WONDEROPOLIS: WHAT IS DIABETES?

https://www.wonderopolis.org/wonder/what-is-diabetes

Read a short overview of diabetes basics at this educational site.

Every effort has been made to ensure that these websites are appropriate for children. However, because of the nature of the Internet, it is impossible to guarantee that these sites will remain active indefinitely or that their contents will not be altered.